THE HAPPINESS
OF THIS WORLD

THE HAPPINESS
OF THIS WORLD

Poems and Prose

KARL KIRCHWEY

A MARIAN WOOD BOOK

Published by G. P. Putnam's Sons

a member of Penguin Group (USA) Inc.

New York

A MARIAN WOOD BOOK
Published by G. P. Putnam's Sons
Publishers Since 1838
a member of the Penguin Group
Penguin Group (USA) Inc., 375 Hudson Street, New York, New York 10014, USA •
Penguin Group (Canada), 90 Eglinton Avenue East, Suite 700, Toronto, Ontario M4P 2Y3,
Canada (a division of Pearson Penguin Canada Inc.) • Penguin Books Ltd, 80 Strand, London
WC2R 0RL, England • Penguin Ireland, 25 St Stephen's Green, Dublin 2, Ireland (a division of
Penguin Books Ltd) • Penguin Group (Australia), 250 Camberwell Road, Camberwell,
Victoria 3124, Australia (a division of Pearson Australia Group Pty Ltd) • Penguin Books
India Pvt Ltd, 11 Community Centre, Panchsheel Park, New Delhi–110 017, India •
Penguin Group (NZ), Cnr Airborne and Rosedale Roads, Albany, Auckland 1310,
New Zealand (a division of Pearson New Zealand Ltd) • Penguin Books
(South Africa) (Pty) Ltd, 24 Sturdee Avenue, Rosebank, Johannesburg 2196, South Africa

Penguin Books Ltd, Registered Offices:
80 Strand, London WC2R 0RL, England

The author gratefully acknowledges permission to quote from the following:

"In Distrust of Merits," from *Collected Poems* by Marianne Moore. Copyright © 1944
by Marianne Moore; copyright renewed © 1972 by Marianne Moore. Reprinted with the permission
of Scribner, an imprint of Simon & Schuster Adult Publishing Group.

Paterson by William Carlos Williams. Copyright © 1946, 1948, 1949, 1951, 1958
by William Carlos Williams. Reprinted with the permission of New Directions.

Library of Congress Cataloging-in-Publication Data

Kirchwey, Karl, date.
The happiness of this world : poems and prose / by Karl Kirchwey.
p.   cm.
"A Marian Wood book."
ISBN 978-0-399-15365-5
I. Title.
PS3561.I684H37   2006   2006040995
811'.54—dc22

Printed in the United States of America
1   3   5   7   9   10   8   6   4   2

Book design by Meighan Cavanaugh

This book is for Rickie Flanders.

CONTENTS

Acknowledgments   *xiii*

The Happiness of This World
(from the French of Christophe Plantin)   *xv*

I. ORIGINAL SONG

Morning   3

Spring Narcissus   4

A Pressed Rose, Being My Father's Gift
to My Mother on the Day I Was Born   5

Fireflies   6

Upon a Lock of His Own Hair,
Kept from the Age of Nineteen Months   7

Mockingbird   8

A Pair of Sterling Silver Shoehorns   9

Garter Snakes   10

A Presto of Schubert's   11

II. AN ANSWERING WIT

Metaphor   15

Blackberries   16

Reading Akhmatova   17

A Sonata of Biber's   18

Sandlot & Tenderloin   20

The News   21

At Giacometti's Grave   22

Black Cat *(from the German of Rainer Maria Rilke)*   26

Road Kill   27

Speedway Feature   29

III. RENDITION

Nocturne, Morningside Heights   33

The War   34

Chases in Arras   37

Homecoming *(after* The Odyssey, *Book XXIII)*   39

After Suetonius   40

Quiet Like the Fog   41

Villanelle   43

The Bonobites   45

Dandelions   47

IV. REPAIR

Val Veddasca   51

Russell's Store   53

Repair   54

Interior with Portrait of Savonarola   56

The Names   58

Tynnichus of Chalcis   60

V. A *YATRA* FOR YAMA   61

Notes   103

*. . . This symbol is used to indicate a stanza break
at the top or bottom of a page.*

ACKNOWLEDGMENTS

Many of the poems in this book, sometimes in different form, have appeared in the following print and electronic journals, to whose editors grateful acknowledgment is made:

The American Scholar: "Morning," "Reading Akhmatova"
Commonweal: "The Happiness of This World" (from the French of Christophe Plantin), "Interior with Portrait of Savonarola," "Road Kill"
Literary Imagination: "After Suetonius," "Black Cat" (from the German of Rainer Maria Rilke), "Waking After One Month Away," "Walking Green Beach Three"
The Nation: "A Prayer to Ganesh"
New England Review: "A Pair of Sterling Silver Shoehorns," "Tynnichus of Chalcis"
The New Republic: "The Names," "Sandlot & Tenderloin"
The Paris Review: "At Giacometti's Grave"
Parnassus: Poetry in Review: "The News," "Val Veddasca," "The War"
The Sewanee Review: "Blackberries," "Homecoming," "Mockingbird," "Russell's Store"

Slate: "Fireflies"

Southwest Review: "Chases in Arras," "Dandelions"

Washington Square: "Metaphor"

Western Humanities Review: "The Bonobites," "Repair"

The Yale Review: "A Pressed Rose, Being My Father's Gift to My Mother on the Day I Was Born," "A Sonata of Biber's"

"Garter Snakes" was included in *Poetry Calendar 2006: 365 Classic and Contemporary Poems / 300 Poets*, issued by Alhambra Publishing.

"The Happiness of This World" first appeared in a broadside sheet from the Aralia Press, for which thanks are due to Michael Peich.

"Nocturne, Morningside Heights" first appeared in *Poetry After 9/11: An Anthology of New York Poets.*

"A *Yatra* for Yama" was written in response to a suggestion by Ben Downing, and appeared, in a shorter version, in *Parnassus: Poetry in Review.* I am indebted to my brother Mike Tompkins for much contained in it. I would also like to acknowledge the cheerful and resourceful companionship of Steven Flanders on the journey described, which was made possible by a faculty research grant from Bryn Mawr College.

To my editor, Marian Wood, goes my deep gratitude, as it does, always, to Tamzen Flanders, who makes the happiness of this world possible.

THE HAPPINESS OF THIS WORLD

To have a house that is commodious, clean and beautiful;
tapestried with fragrant espaliers, a garden;
fruits; excellent wine; a small retinue; few children;
to have, without commotion, a wife who is loyal.

To have no debts, no dalliance, no lawsuits, no quarrel;
no obligation with parents to make division;
to content oneself with little, to hope for no attention
from the great; to scale one's plans to what is manageable.

To live with candor and without ambition;
to give oneself to piety without hesitation;
to damp the passions and make them obedient,

cultivating branch and graft, telling one's Rosary
while preserving a free spirit and a strong judgment:
this is to wait at home for death comfortably.

—FROM THE FRENCH OF CHRISTOPHE PLANTIN (1514–1589)

I.

ORIGINAL SONG

MORNING

Paxil, Xanax, Valium:
as generics, these
are all available to you
at reduced cost,
says the night's e-mail.
My father hated Spam.
My son asks why.
That was the war,
I say. Which war? he wants to know,

and then sets off
in his brilliant fleece,
dodging the blasted yew,
its branches twisted by wind, by frost,
striding into the day
like Gandalf toward Mordor,
his shadow long before him,
and each black needle
flashing with dew.

SPRING NARCISSUS

It catches you like a blow
in one sweet breath from that bed
from which you will never arise:
a mingled odor, naphtha and cannabis;
what your mother laid away each year
in April until she died;
what you were kept to know,
to feel always as trespass
and uncontrollable desire.

A Pressed Rose, Being My Father's Gift to My Mother on the Day I Was Born

Folded in an ancient Kleenex,
     first there were the tiny seeds,
black and shaken from the matrix
     of the unmet spirit's needs.

Then I found thorns, each green virgule
     tender, though, too soft to tear
or snag on the nap of subtle
     distance one kept from the other.

Finally the rusted petals,
     quilted, black as menstrual blood,
crumbled in my palm to metals
     of loneliness and solitude.

I will make this garden flower.
     I will coax one seed to grow,
teach the braided thorns to utter
     why he gave her this, and how.

FIREFLIES

Those nights the fireflies love best—
windless and a little humid—
when they are current in the pasture,
busy in their greeny traffic,
signaling beneath the stars
("Like a club's marquee," she says,
remembering Fifty-second Street),
then I think pleasure is like this,
accomplished in a perfect silence
undeceived by loneliness.

And in the morning on the lawn,
seedpods of Eastern cottonwood
lie scattered open, white and brilliant,
as if true to some child's account
of what pleasure becomes with daylight.

Upon a Lock of His Own Hair,
Kept from the Age of
Nineteen Months

Surely it was some other dauphin, not
the melon-headed tumbledown prince shown
in an Eisenhower-era snapshot,
whose topknot unaccountably gleams on,
bound up in a dim foxed envelope with
dead letters. But whatever inhabits
the lashings of black thread on white-blond just
starting to darken with time, the snicker
of silver it cost, grievous, aroused, both,
is beginning to crown, until you must
forgive those hands that thought, before they went,
to keep what all their love could not prevent.

MOCKINGBIRD

for John Hollander

Dreams of loss and fleeing: then I woke.
My thought reeled like a night-black crazy quilt
in broidered vectors as the mocker spoke,
and I lay numbering the riffs that filled
the maple's groined arch at the break of day:
Passion is risible, grief merely wrong,
and as for what it was you meant to say,
there is no such thing as original song.

But as the light strengthened, a borrowed language
returned for me to do with what I could,
for all the world as if the one true knowledge
weren't irony, or as if I might ride
even on broken wheels through the old patchwork,
take up my still-warm bed and learn to walk.

A Pair of Sterling Silver Shoehorns

Like—well, like stiff twin compasses they lie,
    angled, dust-islanded, on my father's dresser
in an unrecoverable symmetry.
    Not touching, they incline toward each other.

I have seen others fashioned of true horn;
    for these are sterling silver counterfeits.
Yet what affinities there must have been:
    the hush of silk, the shrug of a long foot

into a calfskin pump, the hectic flush,
    the whiff of perfume, the precocious fob
and Phi Bete key—all lost now in the tarnish,
    the tawny gold of sweat where it would cup

the heel briefly: in which I see reflected,
    as in a concave mirror, my own face,
bloated with sounding their attenuated
    desire. They liked to dance; they liked to dress;

and for a while they loved each other, too,
    until the dream, the single ivory nut
cinching their lives, cracked and became untrue
    just where the haft and blade join at the tool's throat.

GARTER SNAKES

August sun warms the great stone of the back step,
     a marble water trough
turned upside down years ago, bone-white and deep,
     chisel-marked and rough.

They wind and unwind from it, black and yellow,
     their red tongues flickering,
subtle and fluent through the grooved hollow
     where a useful stone has found its ending.

The smell of common kitchen-garden spearmint
     rides the translucent hush
of their shed skins through the daylilies' bent
     stems clogged with the ghostlike mesh

and gray drogue of their change. Through hazard colors
     and heated julep shade,
I cannot now recall what was between us,
     or why I should bruise their head.

A Presto of Schubert's

(D. 810, "Death and the Maiden")

One time, in the summer of my
eleventh year, my family
had just moved into a new house
in a suburb where my mother
would recover her old friends, keep

the cigarettes and booze more or
less under control, and even
outwit bedridden depression
for a while. We'd been there a week.
I was upstairs taking a bath.

I had an ear infection from
the pool at the Holiday Inn,
and as I sat amid the flesh-
colored tiles, I heard music I
had never heard before, a rude

. . .

blatting sound that seemed to approach
at the speed of penumbra and
eclipse. At first I thought, *Because
my ear is ill,* and then I thought,
It is like the last word of doom.

The water's face trembled and was
still again, as if nothing had
happened, and I called out to my
mother, and she said it was the
twelve-o'clock horn from the firehouse.

But I had seen the tidy brick
firehouse, with its pots of crimson
geraniums, and it could not
have been the source of the music
I had just heard riding famished

across the landscape, spurred on in
a dotted rhythm of echo
as if somehow to stifle its
own countervailing melody
in pursuit of pure extinction.

Appalled in the dripping quiet,
I lacked words to tell her even
this, nor would I recognize it
until four years after her death
in a late presto of Schubert's.

II.

AN ANSWERING WIT

METAPHOR

A man dressed all in white
strides into a tunnel of gastric silk,
patiently clearing the fouled guys,
beating smooth the crimson folds
before a chuff of flame
causes the sluggish palace to stir and rise,
as if churning a sea of milk.
Or a voice roars inside a bronze bull,
raising the tyrant body past its own thimble
of wickerwork, the red emblem
of its failure, the patchwork of its deeds.
But it is I who am here to tell it,
I who have drunk anything I could read through:
you have never known an emptiness like this.

BLACKBERRIES

Words crushed on the palate end in silence
every time, not in the palaver of song.
You cannot fill your basket with what is merely visible,
grapeshot of onyx, gleaming confected dark,
for here neglect has grown complex and fertile,
in this tangled fane, this daggered understory,
and to pluck the sinister fruit, you must angle in
on a reach with your left arm, neither too shallow
nor too steep, one from which you can recover,
then bear down gently until you feel the parting
of flesh from hollow stem in a place you cannot see.
Your own reflex will always guide you wrong,
your whole hand driven backward onto the thorn,
returned to sunlight with a wounding cursive,
your blood mingling with the pulp of the drupe.
Read what is written there. Discovering
there are seeds between your teeth, speak *that* language.

READING AKHMATOVA

I put the silver key into her palate:
      she's supposed to read aloud to us each day,
      my eight-year-old. *Poems of Akhmatova*
is lying on the bed. She opens it

and starts at random, "Tell me how men kiss you,
      tell me how you kiss." We exchange a glance
      at the widening diction of experience.
No words yet for the Yezhov Terror, though;

none for the cataclysms worked by love,
      the imperative to find an answering wit
      sufficient for the pain of acquiring it.
I am to praise her reading: let it prove

to her there is a self beyond self-hatred.
      More confidently now, she rattles on.
      "What do you want?" The slightest pause, and then,
inexorably, from an age of lead,

the answer comes: "To be with you in hell."
      A lingering silence. She closes the book,
      settling on me with a calm look,
as if I knew a secret and could tell.

A Sonata of Biber's

("Surrexit Christus hodie")

The organ states and restates its plain hymn.
     Again that stubborn
resistance—for I feel it instantly
     rising in me,
entering always with the violin,
striving with it, above, below, within

the 3/2 melody, compelled to grace,
     a sluggishness
awoken to the ancient parable
     and skeptical,
but yielding slowly in the presence of
half-unbelieved-in, half-forgotten love,

which decorates mortality and lends
     to that which ends,
bound now in running figures, now in chords
     breaking towards
a sweetness almost past imagining,
the plangent discipline of each crossed string;

. . .

and though I cannot make a song like this,
   pious and arduous,
its ecstasy expressed in secret halts,
   lingering guilts
appalled or breathing in the silence, yet
I may once listen as the fresh tears start.

Sandlot & Tenderloin

I hooked my fingers through the chain-link fence
      and watched the mound and listened to the chatter.
The tufted infield gave not one true bounce;
      the rutted base paths held wands of rainwater.

And when I came to that other landscape,
      a body as familiar as my own,
the breathlessnesses of its swell and dip,
      velleities of pleasure and aversion,

I wonder what possessed me to look back
      and see him at a window where he was,
spread-eagled by his hunger and a trick
      of light through our drawn shades and watching us.

The News

A perfect evening, Nabokovian
　　　in its mingling of beauty and loss:
　　　a lakeside buffet under pollarded trees
in the courtyard of the Hotel Die Sonne,

the sun expiring in a crimson splurge.
　　　But it was my own sense of culpable
　　　ignorance deepening as we chose our table.
There was some galloping force still at large,

even in that rose-trellised canton:
　　　a woman, her hair in a difficult coiffure,
　　　touching this or that perfect stranger,
speaking a reckless English instead of German,

spoiling to tell of those economies
　　　beyond the hush of gravel, the fume of grillsmoke,
　　　a priestess mad with other human traffic
who sat down in what we thought had been our place.

AT GIACOMETTI'S GRAVE

(BORGONOVO, VAL BREGAGLIA, SWITZERLAND)

To get to this place,
you must go through the village that is above.
If you find yourself before the mountain
or under the bridge, you have gone too far.

Here place is still unmediated by language,
the names prepositional, marked
by the struggle to represent landscape,
which is always elusive, maternal
in the absences for which it compensates us.
His mother lived here her whole life.

The long black dress which touched the ground
troubled me by its mystery; it seemed to be
a part of the body, and that caused
a feeling of fear and confusion.

His wife was given a bolt of rich brocade
that he nailed to their bedroom wall.
From a crack in the wall between his bedroom
and his mother's came cigarette smoke and coughing.
After her death, he would croon to himself
"Alberto, come eat!" in her voice.

. . .

He lies in the cemetery of San Giorgio.
The Maira flows at his head; Sciora rises at his feet.
The big rigs sob down the Maloja road,
rifling onward their cargo of felled, stripped logs.

Between the months of November and March,
the sun does not climb above the mountain wall.
These are the shadow months, the months he loved best,
when the coldest hour is noon.

While working, I've had to eliminate
one color after another;
no: one after another the colors have deserted the party;
at the last there remained only: gray! gray! gray!

The churchyard stone is quarried from the mountain:
quartzite, serpentine, granite.
Someone has put a bunch of bluets
on top of his grave, so I wade into the meadow
to gather pink geraniums.
My pants legs are stained with pollen.

. . .

It's curious that I can't manage
to make what I see. To do that,
one would have to die of it.
If I could actually make a head as it is,
That would mean one can dominate reality.
It would be total knowledge. Life would stop.

He lived in Geneva during the war,
and for five hundred yards around the Hôtel de Rive,
his footsteps were visible
in the plaster dust that fell from his clothes.

Once a church was built at Rome
on the site of a midsummer snowfall.
In the little church of San Giorgio,
the Word of God declares itself unmediated,
free of alien traditions
and human superstitions.

One starts by seeing the person
who poses, but little by little,
all the possible sculptures of him intervene.
The screen between his reality and mine grew thicker.

. . .

He befriended a prostitute
whom he nicknamed "La Grisaille."
He bought her a crimson roadster
in which she drove from Paris
to meet him on the stone bridge.
He would not let her enter his mother's house.

Between the ages of four and seven,
I saw only those things
which could be useful to my pleasure.
These were above all stones and trees.

In his studio there lived a vixen fox
with a feral smell. Her name was Miss Rose.
She made her burrow in a heap of plaster dust,
and the city-bred dogs howled all night for her.

From the high gullies of Sciora
descend queues of dazzling snow.
The Maira River is prone to violence,
but now the stones are white and dry in the sun.

The clock-tower of San Giorgio
is missing all four sets of hands.
Nature creates and forgets
and creates again. O master beyond time,
though I speak to you in color and language,
it is failure that validates the effort.

BLACK CAT

Even a ghost is like a solid place
against which your gaze clangs and heaves;
but there, in that black pelt of nothingness,
your fiercest look somehow merely dissolves:

just as a madman, when he's on a roll,
raves and stamps around in the manic dark
only to break himself on the padded wall,
the rage evaporating from his attack.

It seems that every glance she's ever met
she conceals somewhere deep inside,
the better to toy with it, to vex and threaten
with looking; and finally to sleep with it.
But one time she will turn, as if awakened, with
her face set squarely in the middle of yours:

and there you'll find your own gaze reflected
in the round and lovely stones of her amber eyes,
unlooked for, too, and kept in that prison
like some species of insect long gone from the earth.

—FROM THE GERMAN OF RAINER MARIA RILKE (1875–1926)

Road Kill

Actaeon ripped to gobbets by his hounds,
felled in the mazy paths of venery:
it was not like that. Where the dark abounds,
a five-point buck hit by an SUV
ghosted into my lane with car-wreck sounds,
huge, pale and cartwheeling like an empty
refrigerator box. An antlered gleam
caromed in fragments out of my high beam.

For whoso list to hunt—the hart, the hart—
I thought my Previa took him in her stride,
breasting the rain-slick road, always apart,
not tangled this way, fell and underside
so implicated in a single dart
of time, horn and steel dragging through the pied
landscape and the loud reek of viscera.
I set my hazards and walked back to where

the buck lay broken in the autumn rain,
so beautiful, the pouch of testicles
at ease in pure white fur, and a small stain
of blood at the mouth. I said canticles
of thanks to pure Diana once again:

the windshield had not gone to particles;
the buck had not mounted and, floundering,
killed me with sharp hooves of engendering.

High on the cannon bones I set both hands,
intending to drag him out of the way—
my chance should not become another's chance—
but saw as I did so that he stirred weakly:
the net of breath still held. I lost my balance,
my hands gloved in his musk, and staggered free
of that black gaze diamonded by the rill
at the curb. I could not find even the little

he sought in me, who lacked a simple weapon
to end him with, so that his death was slow,
a long indifference, like the rescission
of splattered leaves, a passion in dumb-show;
and I was wounded down to the white bone,
but somehow quickened by my looking, too,
as if a god had bearded my night-black car
with long white hairs embedded in the rubber.

Speedway Feature

That sound again. It had—come to the window:
what noise or shout was that? It tore the sky,
past the near meadows, over the still stream,
up the hillside. They have backed a jet engine
against a derelict Mercedes and run it up full throttle.
The exhaust gases, at five thousand degrees,
quickly reduce the car to a pool of metal.

III.

RENDITION

. . . we devour
ourselves. The enemy could not
have made a greater breach in our
defenses.

—MARIANNE MOORE, "IN DISTRUST OF MERITS"

I. Leadership passes into empire; empire begets insolence;
    insolence brings ruin.

—WILLIAM CARLOS WILLIAMS, *PATERSON* I, III (AFTER ISOCRATES)

Nocturne, Morningside Heights

Not expunged,
not by the city's ambient light,
the three stars of Orion's belt
cinched tight as a Yankees pitcher's blouse,
the stadium's sink of glow
damped some hours since,
the thread (I did not say threat)
of bridge lights looping frailly east
toward the dawn five hours away,
the muezzin's call
across the green bronze cornices of Harlem
(no, no, the sun will not have seen
anything greater) and, far uptown,
the foursquare garnet constellation
of building lights that blink, solemn,
against a sky empty of planes,
no sob of passage overhead.
The city lies all unprostrated.
It is too early and too late.

(October 2001)

THE WAR

Having survived the European Theater,
        my father shipped home in July of '45.
Passing through Midtown, he looked up and saw
        something amazing, an Army B-25
protruding from the seventy-ninth floor

of the Empire State Building. What were the odds of that?
        He thought for a moment he'd gone Asiatic
under the pressure of imminent redeployment
        to the East, where he might confidently expect
to be killed as his brother had been. But this was different:

contingency came home with Lt. Col. William Smith,
        decorated for one hundred missions over Germany,
on a milk run to Newark from Bedford, Mass., with
        a couple of riders. This was no kamikaze
attack on a flat-top. In the stone trap and labyrinth

of Manhattan, he got lost and crashed his plane, as if
        he'd been saved through combat only for this:
to show an icon vulnerable, not proof;
        to breach its maze of domestic complacencies
(the offices of Catholic War Relief);

. . .

to die in the bright inferno of a star
  at the behest of an invisible will;
to shake a homeland that presumed too far,
  and rouse it from its dreams of useless skill.
All the rest was just telling a good story.

His widow said the night before, their infant son
  had recognized him for the first time (Hector with
  Astyanax);
several were caught in a river of burning gasoline;
  one jumped to his death; the elevator brakes
saved one after falling seventy-five floors. An aircraft engine

hurtled clear across to Thirty-third Street
  and dropped onto the roof of a sculptor's penthouse studio,
demolishing the maquette of a work called *Pro Patria*.
  (The artist was away at the Scarsdale Golf Club, though,
testing a new kind of five-iron he hoped to patent.)

. . .

Archbishop Spellman said the building had been "gored,"
    and with poignant grief, a week before Hiroshima,
he prayed for those whose human hopes lay with the dead.
    My father saw the whole thing as an emblem
of the odds against his ever being spared.

But what am I to make of this later miracle?
    Two pillars of cloud lead us daily,
while fire burns, Solomonic, in the temple,
    unappeased by grief's idolatry.
    Here is the war. Where is the enemy?

CHASES IN ARRAS

Chases in Arras, guilded emptinesse,
Shadows well mounted, dreams in a career,
Embroider'd lyes, nothing between two dishes;
    These are the pleasures here.

—GEORGE HERBERT, "DOTAGE"

At a B&B in sober Ocean Grove
    (Victorian gingerbread architecture and flags),
I was woken from a sound sleep at 1:35
    by a citizen on the boardwalk finding his sea legs

in a lightly embellished version of "The Star-Spangled Banner."
    I tore out half-dressed just as he concluded
and stowed a gleaming trumpet in his car.
    He seemed baffled at how he had offended,

and in the bovine patience of his gaze,
    I saw the dozing Methodist encampment,
and behind it the republic's distances
    westward, outlasting all sustained intent,

. . .

and myself, too, in broken khakis, haggard,
       impeachable, alone. I thought: *Shall I*
bury him with a curse and go back to bed?
       But then I heard the Atlantic, endlessly

tumbling and shuddering out of the darkness,
       advance its famished luminescent edge
to embroider our chases in Arras
       and comprehend them in its ancient deluge.

Homecoming

(after *The Odyssey*, Book XXIII)

After spades had scraped the packed-earth floor
    (the first arrow caught Antinoüs in the throat),
after the air had been purged with fire and sulfur
(the arrow pierced Eurymachus from nipple to liver),
    after the reeking halls had gone silent,
after the maids had used their own tears to water
the sponges and scrub down the lion-clawed furniture
    (the spear entered Leocritus' groin and jutted out),

then he commanded a dance, and Phemius struck his lyre,
and the survivors took up the Phrygian measure,
    men's clean tunics and women's sashes moving to it,
    mesmerized, trampling the spirits of the dead underfoot
as the palace echoed to its farthest corner,
    and he watched them, beneath his eyelids the pupils set
like horn or iron, nothing at their center,

and someone passing in the street outside, a stranger,
    hearing that music, smiled and said, "A wedding banquet!"

AFTER SUETONIUS

The Romans knew that Caesar was a god
because, after the ivory funeral couch
had blazed up and subsided to a char,
after his will had been read, there appeared,
one hour before sunset, a comet which
shone seven days, apotheosizing the dictator.

What rude foot scattered this cremation so?
An Advent sparkle over Palestine, Texas,
forty miles high, twelve thousand miles an hour;
a ragged boom, audible in Nacogdoches;
a ring finger (with ring); a human heart
(not beating); in San Augustine, a blackened torso.
There is no omen, only accident,
imped on the peach-pale wing of our own error.

(FEBRUARY 1, 2003)

Quiet Like the Fog

At evening when the air was cool,
Adam's fall was palpable.

What is that, hoisted on the vernal green
    of steel bridge-trusses?
It is the oldest secret ever seen,
    above the Euphrates.

At evening the white dove came back,
a branch of olive in its beak.

Passion's enigma, self that we despise,
    twisted black and reeking;
image of God we cannot recognize,
    no longer speaking.

O earthward hour, o sacred time:
He bends His Head; we rise to meet Him.

Bark from an ancient tree, mottled with dread,
    set mutely to declare
that love is the younger sibling of hatred,
    if only by an hour.

. . .

Go claim the gift: it has been paid for,
none costlier and none more fair.

At dusk those who came were driven away,
   threatened with death.
But they came back again another day,
   and wrapped it in white cloth.

(APRIL 2004)

Villanelle

(remembering Manadel al-Jamadi, and others)

"They stressed him out so bad he passed away,"
then buried him in ice like Heinekens.
I don't believe a single word they say,

the euphemism of it stubbornly
embedded in the jargon of complacence:
"They stressed him out so bad he passed away,"

rigged up with wires like a Christmas tree,
the hooded man, and threatened into balance.
I don't believe a single word they say,

but photographs tell a more complex lie.
Thumbs-up, the woman soldier points and grins:
"They stressed him out so bad he passed away,"

and images framed in complicity
survive as the most lethal evidence.
I don't believe a single word they say,

. . .

although self-image takes a while to die,
denial so wrought up with impudence.
"They stressed him out so bad he passed away."
I don't believe a single word they say.

(MAY 2004)

THE BONOBITES

So at the utter end of civilization,
it was decided to look to the apes for guidance,
to the bonobos, a kind of pygmy chimpanzee
found only in the Congo River Basin,
with the idea that the two percent of genetic material
distinguishing the human species might have been aberrant.

The world's elder statesmen all came to Kinshasa
for what they could learn, and shook each hairy hand
and gazed deep into the black-skinned wrinkled faces
which honored the female and did not covet property
or conceal true motives under high-sounding rhetoric
or feel another's good fortune as a personal grief.

Above all they wanted to know how to stop making war,
how to stop thinking of one another as less than human,
the victim becoming attached to his torturer.
And when it came time to return to their own countries,
they genuinely wept, and promised one another
that the world would no longer continue as it had been.

There was so much to relearn! The missionary position,
for which natural selection seemed to have adapted them,
the self reflected in the eyes of another;

French kissing and all the varieties of masturbation;
the bared teeth of a grin that arises from anxiety,
and audible laughter, which is how humans share pleasure.

Finally, even without the bright peony of genital swelling,
they came to regard their own constant heat
neither as torment nor as secret shame
nor as a mere evolutionary protection against infanticide,
but rather as all they knew of stability and permanence,
their bodies bound to one another in every limb.

As always, there were those who resisted the change.
Sexual play now began at one year old,
and intercourse at the age of eleven. It was not uncommon
to see people taking pleasure of one another
on railway trains, in restaurants or in public parks,
whenever they felt uncertain or afraid,

and especially in churches, mosques and synagogues.
And though the bonobos had long since passed away
(the World Bank had opened their forest habitat to logging),
for a while, in all the cities of the world,
in all the enamel patchwork of its cultivated fields,
it did seem that a new age of peace was at hand.

DANDELIONS

My daughter, who is nine years old today,
     in her spontaneous delight
returns from the unkempt front lawn to say
        the first generation
        of this year's dandelions is done,
     all gone to seed-heads overnight,
which she with one short breath can blow away.

Her grandmother, still prone to sudden tears,
     lifts her eyes from *The New York Times*
at this news. Her husband of many years
        died back in February.
        A bouquet of the world's folly,
     its elder statesmen's brazen crimes,
keeps her heart passionate, and her gaze clears

as my daughter describes the colonies
     of broad-leafed, lion-maned, chrome-yellow
volunteers. And yet how grimly it must please,
        the round of birth and bale:
        those grayer heads that now prevail
     have waited sylvan ages to
bring this land, like a gardener, to its knees.

(MAY 2005)

IV.

REPAIR

VAL VEDDASCA

L'occhio del padrone ingrassa l'orto.

Adolfo's bought a village in the hills,
a ghost village, all schist and stinging nettles

and fallen hand-hewn beams of forest chestnut
hauled up on men's backs (because at this height

the trees don't grow): but a village entire.
Not since the fifties has anyone lived here,

and then only goatherds in the summer months.
His wife's down in the valley. She's been here once.

Adolfo's threaded a wire necklace with
the pasture's scattering of ruminant teeth—

chamois, deer, ibex—by the candle's glow.
His own teeth are giving him trouble, though.

The doctor's got him on an antibiotic,
so we drink his red wine for him and talk:

. . .

the Northern League, what Martial has to say
about mushrooms (parting with them isn't easy).

Across the valley, lights of villages
come up in their frail loop: Indemini's

first, then Biegno, Lozzo, Armio, Graglio.
Adolfo says they're almost empty now.

Once set at a safe height from valley raiders,
they cling to friable stone's aquifers,

but there's no work. The young people have left;
the old are dying. Adolfo's hands are deft:

now he's carving a bowl of chestnut for me,
reciting from the Ugolino canto of Dante.

Adolfo blows the candle out before bed.
We close the circle of his solitude.

Russell's Store

for Genevieve Werner

You've come for Motrin, since the child's dry cough
      at intervals has kept you up all night.
But what you notice is Parsons Smut-Off
(*Portnoy's Complaint* beside it on the shelf),
      for cleaning oats, potatoes, barley and wheat.

Or say they're at the other end, your troubles:
      you've come for Balmex. But you find instead
straight pins and Yahtzee, Velveeta and thimbles,
next to a copy of Nostradamus' *Oracles,*
      one book among many you have not read.

You've come in, not for news (a conquering army,
      far from this tranquil Catskill mountain town,
has killed civilians inadvertently),
and not for that dog-eared *The Praise of Folly,*
      but for the First Strike matches it leans on.

But even if you leave without what you came for,
      your visit here somehow outwits the day's
routine exhaustion. Through the broken screen door,
parent, Promethean, sleepless voyager,
      you find you have grown wiser than Erasmus.

REPAIR

The parquet has become all sinks and man-traps,
      deep-rutted by the feet of kitchen chairs.
The wagging tongue-and-groove laps—overlaps—
      its generations of mismatched veneers.

The beveled oak moldings are fanged with nails
      half drawn by the concussion of existence;
each saddle's ridden up, under your footfalls,
      which you counted as a firm threshold once.

The eggshell wall's gone to a maculate
      moue and pucker; the cabinet door's
top hinge is double-jointed, so that it
      shows off just like a schoolboy during recess.

Still, for a few moments the westering sun
      catches the window opposite and, glancing,
touches the butcher-block (its sealant gone)
      and makes it glow in a radiant oblong,

. . .

insisting that the ordinary be given its due,
    the gimcrack habitude of every day.
Years pass, and things acquire a bias, and you—
    so deep in life you did not notice—may

yet honor, from a kind of present exile,
    this well-loved place in which no line is plumb;
or know it with leaving, since after all
    to repair is also to be called home.

INTERIOR WITH PORTRAIT OF SAVONAROLA

The winter sun,
angling across the south pasture,
catches his mason jar
where it waits on the windowsill,
mute and rimed with uric salts,
and makes it glitter.
It is too late to speak of faults.
It is too late to be bitter.
The woodstove's cold; the desk is closed;
the high carved bed seems narrow
to have kept them both so long,
and at its foot's a cedar chest
containing linen she air-dried
and folded away sweet last summer.
On the wall's a unicorn
in white pastel, done by their last-born;
a crow perched on a tree; a golden-haired angel
and (more of his whimsy)
Savonarola in profile,
who said, "My purposes were few,
but they were great."
Before they burned Savonarola,
they scratched his fingernails with glass:
the frost-flowers on the window grow like that,

like purposes. Darkness is streaming
from the priest's habit,
the feathers of the crow,
fed by the jar's crystal mouth,
the glazed flank of the bed,
the concealed smile of linen.

The Names

It satisfied desire and created desire.

—Bernard DeVoto

for my sister

All night it kept up its music, the Boulder River,
      skirmishing across a shallow bed of stones
beyond the cottonwood, Russian olive and poplar,
      the tangled mosquitoey woods where cattle browse.

Cabled in its quick places, glassy in its deep,
      the river had no particular claim on me
(though I have known other rivers that did),
      except that it inhabited my sleep,

not with *Multnomah, Rejone* or *Mississury,*
      the steady incantation of lost names,
not even with the pounding of the Burlington Northern Santa Fe
      eastward with its load of chemicals and coal,

. . .

but with something more fugitive and unpronounceable,
    something I glimpsed in the vestments of the Audubon's
    warbler,
black and yellow and white and once again black,
    then lost through the dry grass and rubbed sage of
    midsummer.

TYNNICHUS OF CHALCIS

When you find you have left your warm bed
        to sit befuddled in the rising dawn,
                sniffing its laced odors of bonemeal and dew;

when your spirit swims into its level
        like the horizon's line of orange char
                and your heart slows from where it was it drove

while you were a citizen of dream's republic;
        when you listen to the bird's iterated tonic
                through the semitones of green, then for
                heaven's love

remember Tynnichus the poet of Chalcis,
        who never composed anything worth recall,
                according to Socrates, until, possessed,

he uttered a single immortal lyric of praise,
        a lifetime's bondage yielding this return,
                halting, stiff and chilled, waiting like you
        beneath a sky of unrepeatable azure.

V.

A Yatra for Yama

in memory of Peter Flanders

I.

I have them on the desk in front of me now, manila file folders with a faint and indescribable smell about them, compounded of the mildew of sixty years of humid Connecticut summers, of typewriter ink and old paper and the dried perspiration of those who wrote the letters these folders contain and the dried tears of those who received them, back when the suddenness of a letter received by surface mail could be sufficient to prompt tears. (I have never wept over an e-mail.) It is an attar of the past that seems to deepen and open out to the point of vertigo as I inhale it, at once familiar and strange, until I am balanced perfectly between intoxication and dread. These folders do not abide a casual attention; the past asserts itself in them as an imperative and a challenge. For to travel back into the past is to contemplate one's own extinction as well as that of one's ancestors.

In the National Museum in Phnom Penh, Cambodia, there is a motto spelled out in small rounded stones at the feet of an image of the Buddha: YOU SHOULD ABANDON ORIGINS.

In one of the manila folders, there is a Western Union telegram, dated July 11, 1944. It was delivered to my paternal grandmother. It reads:

THE NAVY DEPARTMENT DEEPLY REGRETS TO INFORM YOU THAT YOUR SON LIEUTENANT (JG) KARL WENDELL KIRCHWEY JR USNR IS MISSING FOLLOWING ACTION IN THE PERFORMANCE OF HIS DUTY AND IN THE SERVICE OF HIS COUNTRY. THE DEPARTMENT APPRECIATES YOUR GREAT ANXIETY BUT DETAILS NOT NOW AVAILABLE AND DELAY IN RECEIPT THEREOF MUST NECESSARILY BE EXPECTED. TO PREVENT POSSIBLE AID TO OUR ENEMIES PLEASE DO NOT DIVULGE THE NAME OF HIS SHIP OR STATION.

VICE ADMIRAL RANDALL JACOBS
THE CHIEF OF NAVAL PERSONNEL

The strips of teletype have yellowed less than the half-page on which they were glued; the violet ink is still clear and legible more than sixty years later. I wonder: What was my grandmother doing when she received this telegram? What were her last thoughts before answering the door? It is a situational cliché, the arrival of bad news in this way, made so by many B movies. Steven Spielberg, popularizer and sentimentalist that he is, touched on it in *Saving Private Ryan*; Norman Rockwell would have painted it, if he hadn't been so dedicated to good news. But for my family the consequences of the arrival of this telegram were not what might have been predicted.

The uncle for whom I am named, my father's younger brother by eighteen months, was his mother's favorite. He sculpted, painted, and played the violin; she preserved one of his musical compositions and one of his sculptures, a headless, armless nude female figure. There were life studies behind that sculpture: flying and eros are linked not just in the subconscious. After a disciplinary infraction (parietals) at Harvard, he was told to redeem himself through good works before returning to school. He worked at an aircraft plant and learned to fly, then joined the United States Naval Reserve (USNR). He trained as a fighter pilot at Squantum, Pensacola, and Corpus Christi, and in October 1943 he shipped out for the Pacific aboard the aircraft carrier USS *Enterprise* with Fighting Squadron Ten, known as the Grim Reapers. Their logo was a diving skeleton in helmet and flying goggles, wielding a scythe. My uncle flew state-of-the-art aircraft, first an F4F Wildcat and then an F6F Hellcat. The latter plane, in particular, had been designed specifically to outperform the Japanese Zero fighter, and was heavily armor-plated, with a bulletproof windshield to protect the pilot. A Navy pilot is said to have remarked, "I love this airplane so much that if it could cook I'd marry it."

My father was the dutiful son. Like my namesake, he was well liked by everyone, but he lacked what seems to have been his younger brother's Icarian flair. His eyesight wasn't good enough for him to become a pilot. Instead, he prepared pilots for the Army Air Force on Link trainers until he couldn't stand the boredom anymore. Then he learned German and trained as a radio voice-intercept operator. In the fall of 1944, he sailed for England aboard the *Queen Mary,* and between October of that year and April 1945 he flew twenty-one missions over Europe in the B-24, the heavy bomber known (with military irony) as the Liberator. The regular crew members disliked bringing him along: he added weight to the plane. The Luftwaffe had been more or less crippled by that time, but the missions were not without hazard. A copilot on one flight was beheaded by a cannon shell from a German fighter; ten years later my father would still wake screaming from nightmares. He resolved that if he got out of the service alive, he would mount under glass the silk escape maps that were sewn into his flying suit. (These maps I now have on my living room wall.) He was sent back to the States for redeployment to the Pacific Theater in the summer of 1945, but then the bombs were dropped on Hiroshima and Nagasaki. The planes that dropped them were launched from the very islands his brother had died trying to wrest from the Japanese.

His mother never forgave him for coming home alive when his brother had not. "My life ended the day your brother died," she said to my father.

Teucer

Remember Teucer, mustered out at last,
after the war. His glorious brother Ajax

has killed himself; the bastard brother's just
grateful to be alive. So his ship docks,
and Teucer finds his father Telamon—
who banishes him instantly, because
as far as he's concerned, it's the wrong son
who's staggered home from Troy's far slaughterhouse.
And so it was for you in '45,
your younger brother missing for a year
in the Pacific: baffled by the furious
malignancy with which your mother drove
you from her garden's dahlias and larkspur
to found, in exile, your own Salamis.

The wounding my father received from his mother seemed to make him withdraw into some remote part of himself. When illness had worn him down, at the end of his life, there were moments of astounding emotional exposure: a passionate man dwelt within this innocuous and gentle person. But he would lead my mother and all those around him on a painful emotional chase (the quarry: his own true feelings) that would finally isolate the family in which I grew up. Though I was not exempt from his remoteness, I always felt his warmth and never doubted his love, perhaps because I bore his brother's name.

The next document in the manila folder is a typed letter dated one day before the telegram, July 10, 1944, and headed "Fleet Post Office, San Francisco, California." Written by Roland W.

Schumann, Jr., Lieutenant Commander, U.S. Navy, and once again addressed to my grandmother, it reads, in part:

> As your son Karl's squadron commander, I am writing to extend to you the deep sympathy of the squadron and to amplify as far as possible the official notification which you have received. The uncertainty of the term 'missing in action' is worse than knowing all the facts, so I will tell you what happened as well as I can.
>
> Karl was a member of a four plane flight assigned to protect an observation plane, directing amphibious operations against a Japanese base in the Pacific. The nature of the flight was hazardous, as the planes were over enemy territory at a low altitude. As the flight made a turn over the beach, Ensign Glen Avery, Karl's wingman, saw an anti-aircraft shell explode close to Karl's plane. The plane swerved and went into a dive, striking the water about a mile from shore. The other three planes were not able to follow Karl down at once but the pilots are sure that he did not get out of the plane. When the area of the crash was searched, there was no trace of a life raft or survivor. . . .
>
> I would like to say that there is some hope for his recovery but only through a miracle could he be alive today. . . .

Again that vertigo, as the narrative of the past takes over. I run it like a grainy black-and-white film clip. I tell it like the one hundred nine *rudraksha* beads I wear around my neck, sacred to Shiva, who is creator and destroyer both. It is as secret as guilt in my head: a buzzing arc of black smoke, a tremendous plume of sea-water, then nothing. The outcome is always the same. It is part of who I am.

The "Japanese base in the Pacific" that Commander Schumann is unable to name is the island of Saipan in the Northern Marianas, which the Japanese regarded as their last perimeter before the home islands and therefore a location to be defended at all cost. About this they were correct: from the coral runways of Saipan and nearby Tinian, American bombers, directed by General Curtis LeMay, destroyed enormous acreages of the principal Japanese cities during repeated raids that make the firebombing of Dresden look like a minor harassment.

Though it was overshadowed in history by the D-Day landings in Normandy, which had taken place a little more than a week before, the invasion of Saipan was a huge logistical challenge and one of the great amphibious landings of military history, involving 535 American ships and more than 127,000 troops, all brought from the nearest advance base at Eniwetok, more than a thousand miles away. My uncle died on the first morning of the American assault on Saipan, on June 15, 1944.

Miracles *did* happen. Two days before the landings on Saipan, Commander William I. Martin, pilot of a dive-bomber flying off the *Enterprise,* was shot down by antiaircraft fire over the lagoon. Samuel Eliot Morison tells the story in his monumental *History of United States Naval Operations in World War II.* Martin's two fellow crew members plunged to their deaths. His own parachute failed to open until the last moment, but remembering the experience of another pilot, who survived a fall without a parachute, Martin straightened his body as he hit the water, and landed unhurt in the lagoon. He managed to avoid Japanese fire from the shore, and tugging the seat pack containing his life raft, he scrambled across the reef to open water. He inflated his life raft and used his parachute as a sail, watching shells from the American battleships far offshore pass overhead on their way to Japanese positions on the island. Spotted by American planes, Martin was eventually picked up and taken to the USS *Indianapolis*.

Why, my grandmother must have wondered, could such a miracle not have happened *for her*? My uncle remained where he had fallen, though his location was never further specified. Presumably, his plane lies somewhere off the three-mile-long invasion beach. Even if I were able to persuade the undersea explorer Robert Ballard—who found *PT-109*, John F. Kennedy's boat—to mount a search for the one plane that was my uncle's, amid the immense detritus of war, what would I find? Nothing but an empty tomb.

Our love requires a body, and so does our grief. Without a body, imagination weaves baroque shapes around the absence. Just as depths of water magnify, so the simple facts of my uncle's death have passed, over the years, into myth. He lives larger in my imagination than he could ever have done if he had not died at twenty-two. I have often wondered what role he played in my becoming a poet. There can be no one more forcibly aware of the laws of the physical universe than a pilot; and yet he was said to be artistic.

Perhaps it is this unlikely combination that obsesses me, and not just the Icarian myth.

He lived on in this way for my father and my grandmother, too, until their own deaths. For my grandmother, he represented youth and beauty and promise and even romantic love, given her two unhappy marriages. Their relationship had Oedipal or Lawrentian intensities that neither originated nor ended with his death. For my father, he was a beloved younger brother, but also the object of survivor's guilt, envy, and perhaps even hatred—he was the golden boy to whom my father could never measure up.

While the fact of his fall cannot change, its circumstances, being part of history, are subject to revision. Like those Roman centurions pensioned off on the vineyarded slopes of what is today Lake Geneva in Switzerland, there are pilots alive today—a dwindling number of them—who flew at Saipan with my uncle, and who have found balm for their fading senses in the gentle climates of Florida and California. Over the Internet, I met several of these veterans, some still bearing cartoon-character nicknames, and from them I heard an alternative version of what happened to my uncle. According to this version, he was not killed by Japanese anti-aircraft fire at all, because he was not flying close air support that morning, which is what would have put him over the island and therefore within range of the Japanese guns. Instead, he was flying escort and, though certainly at low altitude, was over the sea. In this version, he was killed probably by "friendly fire" from an American destroyer offshore.

YOU SHOULD ABANDON ORIGINS, says the Buddha. But I cannot do it. The ancestors are jealous: they and their changing stories will not leave me alone. "Aram vult nemus," wrote Ezra Pound in the great first Pisan Canto, also marked by the Second World War: "The grove needs an altar." I try to fill the absence with facts. But the interpretation of those facts changes under my fingers, even if there is no one left alive for me to startle with the news that my uncle may have been killed by his own side. Would such a revelation—that her best-loved son had not died an uncomplicated hero's death—have changed my grandmother's feelings toward my father? Would this, in turn, have made my father less emotionally remote?

At the temple of Ta Prohm, part of the Angkor complex in Cambodia, there is a pediment depicting an episode in the life of the Buddha known as the Great Departure. To find it, you must thread a labyrinth of gigantic silk-cotton roots and skewed walls to a pile of tumbled sandstone blocks. Teetering atop these, you are rewarded with a view of the pediment. Time has rendered the rows of carved figures vivid green with moss. The young Prince Siddhartha is shown leaving his palace by night to begin his quest for enlightenment, celestial figures muffling the hooves of his horse so that he will not wake his wife Yasodhara or his son Rahula.

But most of us cannot so easily leave our families or our past behind.

II.

Today, the island of Saipan is American territory, part of the
Commonwealth of the Northern Mariana Islands. It is fifteen
hours ahead of the mainland and 3,800 miles west of Hawaii. I
arrived after more than twenty hours in the air, my internal clock
and calendar entirely disoriented.

Just as East Coast Americans hop on a plane to the Caribbean,
Japanese, Koreans, and Chinese flock to Saipan for their beach va-
cations. Shop signs are in a variety of languages, though the sign
in the Internet café was in English: "Betel nut chewing is not
permitted." There is something of a boomtown atmosphere about
Saipan, but it overlies a landscape still riddled with the marks of
war, and development appears to be largely unregulated. The con-
crete shells of hotels for which financing has collapsed are prom-
inent, and along the western shore road, pawnshops and gaming
parlors predominate. The garment industry is the second pillar of
the Saipan economy, after tourism, but the opening of mainland
American markets to Chinese imports is causing many factories
to close. Young Chinese women stranded on the island sometimes
resort to "massage" parlors in order to get by.

My hotel, the Pacific Gardenia, backed directly onto the beach
(Sector Blue 2) where the Americans landed in 1944. While wait-
ing for the pizza and beer I'd ordered at a palm-thatch cabana, I
gazed across the lagoon at the eight-story-high cargo ships beyond
the reef, trying to imagine the inferno that American warships
had ignited for the Japanese defenders of the island. During a single

day's firing in advance of the invasion, the seven battleships and eleven destroyers stationed offshore expended 15,000 shells.

I suppose I hoped to find my uncle on Saipan, not in any literal way, of course, but spiritually. Though my father traveled regularly to Asia on business near the end of his career, no one from my family had ever been to Saipan. I bear my uncle's name, and I felt an obligation. My first night on the island, however, I dreamed not of him but of a Black Angus steer hung upside down in a slaughterhouse. I watched as its throat was cut.

The next morning I met Gordon Marciano, my guide for a tour of the military sites on the island. Though he is Chamorro (the island's indigenous population) on his mother's side, his father's family came from the Caroline Islands, to the south of Saipan. He told me, coincidentally, that the Caroline Islanders were brought to Tinian, the smaller island just across a strait from Saipan (it was from Tinian that the *Enola Gay* took off for Hiroshima), to work as beef-slaughterers for the Spanish. But magic, including the magic of coincidence, is taken for granted by the people of Saipan. Gordon told me that his paternal grandfather had the ability to make the rain start or stop. This same grandfather had provided intelligence to the United States during the war, working with a Japanese friend. Gordon's other grandfather, half Chamorro and half Japanese, was crucified by the Japanese but survived. Such anecdotes give some idea of the complexity of the allegiances that prevailed on the island during the war. (Even today it is caught up in the wars of Great Powers: a significant number of young people from Saipan, having enlisted in the Reserve, are in Iraq, giving rise to a new generation of bereaved families.)

The Japanese experience of the American landings was one of unmitigated horror. Whereas American losses on Saipan numbered approximately 3,500, more than 28,000 Japanese soldiers—almost the entire garrison—plus 22,000 Japanese civilians died in the attack. Non-Japanese residents of the island tried simply to avoid being ground to bits between the opposing forces. In a memoir the more valuable for being so completely unselfconscious, an ordinary sailor named James Fahey describes the bombardment of Saipan as it appeared from the deck of the destroyer USS *Montpelier*: "It was like a movie. Big alcohol plants were blown sky high, assembly plants, oil storage plants, ammunition dumps, miles of sugar cane, buildings, railroads, trains, trucks, etc., not to mention . . . thousands of troops, planes, tanks, airfields. . . . I never saw anything like it before, it was like the great Chicago fire." For his part, Samuel Eliot Morison, who served in the Marianas campaign, writes: "There are few things prettier than a naval bombardment, providing one is on the sending not the receiving end and (as in this case) has lost all feeling of compassion for the human victims."

In his more impartial book *The Rising Sun: The Decline and Fall of the Japanese Empire, 1936–1945,* John Toland describes the experience of the young volunteer nurse Shizuko Miura: "As the explosions moved closer she helped transfer those wounded in the earlier shelling to a dugout. . . . Shizuko thought calmly, I have lived for eighteen years and my time to die has come. A shell shook the dugout like an earthquake and knocked her to the ground. . . . She saw a piece of red metal—it was shrapnel—and, curious, touched it with her finger. It burned her. . . . The heat was so intense that she could hardly breathe. She started to make her way through the rubbled streets strewn with bodies." It occurs to me that Shizuko Miura was four years younger than my uncle, in the air above her: the actors in this scene from Armageddon were, many of them, very young.

On July 9, 1944, the Americans announced that Saipan was officially secured. By the end, squeezed onto the cliffs at the north part of the island, civilians were being forced to commit suicide along with Japanese soldiers. The reporter Robert Sherrod quotes the officer of a minesweeper that was operating off the west coast of Saipan: "The sea is so congested with floating bodies we can't avoid running them down. There was one woman in khaki trousers and a white polka-dot blouse, with her black hair streaming in the water. I'm afraid every time I see that kind of a blouse, I'll think of that woman. There was another one, nude, who had drowned herself while giving birth to a baby."

YOU SHOULD KNOW SUFFERING, says another motto spelled out n rounded stones at the feet of the Buddha in the National Museum in Phnom Penh.

On the black granite wall of a cenotaph in the American Memorial Park, I found my uncle, his first name replaced by another: he is listed as Earl Kirchwey.

And that was as close as I got to him, though there was one other encounter, which took place as I walked along the invasion beach on my last day on the island.

Walking Green Beach Three

What did I think to find?
No one alive
could tell me where he fell
or where he lay,
beneath the clear waters
of the Philippine Sea:
so I had traveled
halfway round the world
to find nothing—

except that somewhere
on that beach,
I came into a zone
of such deep calm
I thought perhaps, after all,
he was within my reach,
as the breakers
out past the lagoon
threw up their little hands,

. . .

flung their elbows out
and in the raking light
of afternoon
turned away their face,
unable to decide
whether to applaud
or to deplore
my having come
in the first place.

I looked down at my feet and found something resembling a fulgurite, a knobby thin cylindrical thing. It was a fifty-caliber cartridge casing, a shell that the sand and coral had decorated for sixty years. I had promised my twelve-year-old son, a shell collector, that I would bring him a shell from this beach, but there was no Miraculous Thatcher, no Textile Cone or Venus Comb Murex, no Precious Wentletrap to be found. I slipped this other shell into my pocket.

III.

My father's cautiousness manifested itself in a reluctance to throw anything away. At the time of his death in 1988, his basement contained several ragged cardboard boxes in which the correspondence of many years (including the correspondence about my uncle) had been tumbled by time and repeated family moves. I rescued these boxes, and began a long-term project of organizing this family correspondence. It was not until the late 1990s that several letters from a woman named Martha Ann ("Penny") Gans appeared out of the welter, some addressed to my dead uncle and some to my paternal grandmother. From them I learned that Penny and my uncle would perhaps have married if he had returned from the Pacific. She was a WAC during the Second World War, then went on to a diplomatic career in the Far East, staying in touch with my grandmother for many years after the end of the war. Coincidentally, she was a graduate of Bryn Mawr College, where I began teaching in 2000. Through the Alumnae Office, I learned that she had died in the mid-1990s, so I never had a chance to meet her and ask her about my uncle. I do, however, have something of hers. In the early 1980s, age and illness had forced my grandmother to leave the stone cottage where she had lived for many years, and one of the things I salvaged on that occasion was a charcoal rubbing from Angkor Wat, the largest and most famous temple of the Cambodian complex. Penny had sent it to my grandmother as a souvenir.

For a long time, I know very little about the temples at Angkor. I did not know, for example, from exactly which bas-relief, among the thousands of running feet of sculpture at Angkor Wat, Penny Gans had taken the rubbing. It showed an unsmiling prince with drooping earlobes, sitting cross-legged on the back of an elephant. The rails of a chariot back, a spoked wheel, the splendidly arched neck of a cavalry horse, the raised weapons of foot soldiers: the scene was violently alive. Heedlessly I cut it down to a standard size and put it in a cheap frame. Years later, I would have it properly matted, floated, and framed. Today, like my father's escape maps, the rubbing is on the living room wall in my house. It provided my first exposure to Cambodia, or at least to the golden age of Khmer art, contemporaneous with the building of the great French cathedrals.

My second came in the spring of 1998. I had just taught the last class of a seminar at Yale. Wanting to reward myself, I was browsing in a New Haven bookstore when I came upon Ben Kiernan's *The Pol Pot Regime: Race, Power, and Genocide in Cambodia under the Khmer Rouge, 1975–79*. It must have been the instinct that sometimes drives us to investigate a place or an experience at the opposite pole from our own that made me buy the book and read it. But perhaps the more deliberate accident of my finding the temple rubbing made it inevitable that I should learn more about Cambodia's recent history. Like Saipan, Cambodia had become an imaginary habitation for me, and a real-life place, both exotic and sinister, that I hoped one day to visit.

Angkor Wat is the largest religious structure in the world. Built between 1113 and 1150, it is a rectangle measuring 1.5 by 1.3 kilometers, for an area of almost two hundred hectares. It is a state temple dedicated to Vishnu, but its largest entrance faces west, not east, and it may also have been a funerary temple. In *A History of Cambodia*, David P. Chandler suggests that its bas-reliefs (more than a mile of them) must be followed in counterclockwise rather than in the more usual clockwise direction. He writes, "The reverse direction was usually associated with the dead; so was the west. . . . The word for 'west' in modern Khmer also means 'sink' or 'drown.'" He goes on to describe the work of Eleanor Moron (Mannika), who studied the dimensions of the temple using the unit of measure the Khmer had used, the *hat* (approximately 0.4 meters or seventeen inches), and discovered that certain distances correspond, both in their numbers and in their proportional relationship (4:3:2:1), to the years of the four ages, or *yuga*s, of Indian thought. (We are now in the last—and worst—age, the Kali Yuga, after which the universe will be destroyed and re-created by Brahma.) Chandler concludes: "The distances that a person entering the temple will traverse coincide with the eras that the visitor is metaphorically living through en route to the statue of Vishnu in the central tower. Walking forward and away from the west, which is the direction of death, the visitor moves backward into time, approaching the moment when the Indians proposed that time began." According to this schema, I could walk back into the past and toward my ancestors without inevitably walking toward my own death, as I had feared when I sat in front of the manila folders.

Prominent among the bas-reliefs at Angkor Wat is a wall almost two hundred feet long depicting the Hindu god of death, Yama. He has eighteen arms, and in each hand he holds a club. Assisted by his henchmen Dharma and Chitragupta, he judges souls and sends them to heaven or to the torments of various hells, vividly depicted. Demons with pincers pull out the tongues of thieves and stuff their feet into their mouths. False witnesses are skinned alive, hung from trees, and ground in a mortar. Seducers are torn apart by raptors and thrown into a lake of pus. Gluttons are sawn in half. There is a frozen hell, too, as if Dante and the anonymous sculptors who carved this bas-relief for King Suryavarman II were thinking along the same lines (though half a world and a century and a half apart). In the last punishment shown, demons drive nails into every inch of the bodies of three sinners crucified on frames.

Again that motto spelled out in river stones at the feet of the Buddha in the sunny courtyard of the National Museum in Phnom Penh: YOU SHOULD KNOW SUFFERING. And not far from it is an inscription by the Chinese diplomat Say Fong, describing Jayavarman VII, the great builder king who followed Suryavarman II: "Seeing that his kingdom, which his wisdom had transformed into heaven on earth, was oppressed by death, he produced a divine elixir that brought immortality to all." This must have been *amrita,* the elixir of immortality, which gods and demons momentarily combined their efforts to produce, churning it from the Ocean of Milk. The scene is depicted in Angkor Wat's most famous bas-relief. And there, on my last day at Angkor, I found the prince on his elephant. I had seen so many miles of sculpture, here and at other temples over the previous five days, that I had almost given up on finding him.

As it turns out, he is not a prince but an *asura,* or demon, at the very periphery of figures being recruited to help make *amrita.* (In the end, the gods went back on their word to share the potion. The one demon who managed to take a sip was cut in half by Vishnu, his head becoming Rahu and his tail Ketu—two of the nine planets in the Hindu system of astronomy.) Looking at the sculpture while the tourists flooded past, I felt once again a zone of calm: I had closed a kind of narrative circle on that long-ago gift to my grandmother. The *asura* was at least four feet off the floor. Today visitors are not allowed to touch the wall, but even fifty years ago it cannot have been easy for Penny Gans to make that rubbing.

Angkor Wat

In Cambodia it is called *poot*,
    corn boiled in its own husk
    at the roadside where the red dust
stands in veils. It is salt and sweet:

perhaps the Ocean of Milk
    tasted something like this
    when Vishnu dreamed the cosmos
and gods and demons shared the work

of churning the elixir of immortality
    until they betrayed each other,
    as the monkeys now bicker
and spit kernels. But imagine it differently:

take a cob from the roadside filth;
    take five cobs and make a quincunx
    beside the black iron cauldrons
(the monkeys hissing with wrath),

. . .

by the palm-sugar packets and betel,
    the whiskey bottles of gasoline in rows
    and, wrapped in checked kerchiefs, faces
composed before the day's heat.

There you will find Shiva's stronghold,
    all the inward eye sees, all that thought
    tends toward: Mount Meru, Angkor Wat,
lingam and yoni and the secret of the world.

If the bas-reliefs at Angkor Wat detail the punishment of the guilty, modern Cambodia perfected, as genocide, the punishment of the innocent. Between the years 1975 and 1979—three years, eight months, and twenty days, as any adult alive in Cambodia today will tell you with mathematical precision—the Khmer Rouge caused the death of at least a million and a half Cambodians, out of a population of eight million. There were 343 known killing sites in the country and 19,440 mass graves. The mind yields to numbness when confronted with such numbers.

To the discomfort of some Cambodians, the detention and torture center called Tuol Sleng—originally a high school—has been turned into a genocide museum and is now a stop on the standard tourist circuit. Even its name is ominous: *tuol* means "mound" or "hill," while *sleng* (which can be either an adjective or a noun) means "supplying guilt" or "bearing poison," or else refers to the two kinds of poisonous trees indigenous to Cambodia.

Some classrooms at Tuol Sleng were crudely partitioned with concrete and cinder blocks to make a beehive of tiny cells. For mass detention, lengths of rebar were threaded through shackles dating from the French colonial period. Prisoners defecated into ammunition boxes. Barbed wire was tacked over the building's pleasant balconies so that prisoners would not be able to commit suicide by jumping. The ground-floor rooms were kept as torture chambers. Prisoners were shackled to iron bedsteads like those you might find in some modest provincial hotel. One can almost imagine waking to see the simple designs worked into their headboards, whether the mirrored S's of a balcony railing, or a rising sun, or the f-hole of a musical instrument,

like this   and this   and this.

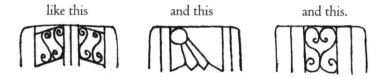

The motto of the Chinese communists at Jiangxi in the 1930s had been: "Better to kill a hundred innocent people than let one truly guilty person go free." The Khmer Rouge declared that you must kill children as well as adults, just as you must kill the root to kill the tree. (They had a taste for natural metaphors: "You are the eyes of Angkar [the Organization]," ran one slogan, "like the eyes of the pineapple.") But children were also pressed into service as jailers. Child guards were particularly feared by the prisoners, because they had no morality and no compassion. Each year the children recruited as guards for Tuol Sleng the year before would be killed by a new generation, so that there would be no witnesses.

In the visitors' book at Tuol Sleng, an Irish tourist had written, "The Americans did it." I had read William Shawcross' *Sideshow: Kissinger, Nixon and the Destruction of Cambodia*, which suggests the same thing: that the merciless, clandestine, and illegal bombing of the country had much to do with establishing the savagery and intransigence of the Khmer Rouge.

Sideshow *by Firelight*

In the first of the autumn rains,
    a tree has fallen tonight
across the power lines,
    so I'm reading *Sideshow* by firelight.

Prince Sihanouk lived well in Beijing,
    with gooseberries and guinea fowl
and nine chefs to do his bidding,
    any cuisine at all.

But they cut out Lon Nil's liver
    and had it cooked in a restaurant
and ate it, each Khmer Rouge soldier.
    He was the brother of the president.

It stretches, the luxurious self,
    and notes its escape from the storm

in a sensible apostrophe
          (*I am dry I am safe I am warm*),

and reads, with a sluggish marvel,
          the words of the old story:
"It takes time, the unconstitutional;
          but the illegal we do immediately,"

how a Cambodian peasant wedding
          was boxed by B-52s,
and bombs in a thirty-ton string
          killed them at their joys.

Imperceptibly it changes,
          the quality of the dark.
The rain is convulsive, tremulous
          on the windows and the attic.

The wind drives on from the east
          with its lashings and its yearning.
Though day will come, and the rest,
          there will be no light by morning.

IGNORANCE IS THE ENEMY OF LIFE, runs another motto, this one
for some reason in French, spelled out in river-rounded stones at
the feet of the Buddha. Why is it that even the most inarguable
assertion can take on a darker resonance in Cambodia? In *Pol Pot:*

Anatomy of a Nightmare, Philip Short tells of an inscription, in both Khmer and French, on either side of the main entrance to the National Library in Phnom Penh: "Force binds for a time; ideas enchain forever." Facts cannot fill the absence, but they can deepen the guilt of ignorance.

In the late summer of 2004, my father-in-law, a brilliant, eccentric musicologist, choral conductor, and amateur cellist, was diagnosed with leukemia. With a methodical patience and fortitude entirely characteristic of him, he set about saying good-bye to the world and those in it he loved. After celebrating his seventy-eighth birthday in September, he was set back by a bout of pneumonia and a stroke later in the fall, but was well enough to be with the family for Christmas. In the depths of New York winter, I left him in frail but stable health to begin my journey, my mother-in-law massaging his feet as he lay on the sofa.

I was in the back of a hired car in the Cambodian countryside, in the company of my father-in-law's younger brother, when our driver, Cheth, received a cell-phone call from an American woman. This was not remarkable: he was often on the phone, lining up work. I looked out the window. Naked children were being bathed with water from communal wells; a father combed his daughter's hair; poultry and livestock moved in and out of the space under stilted palm-thatch huts. I noticed also that bamboo tubes were leaned up against the flowers of the sugar palm to drain off their nectar. This would be boiled for hours, then sold in little palm-leaf packets. Cheth had stopped one day and offered to buy me a packet so that I could taste palm sugar, but fearful that it might contain infected water, I refused his kindness.

We were on our way toward the Kulen mountains, to a place called Kbal Spean, where in 1968 a French archaeologist discovered sculptures of Vishnu cut into the bed of a river, to be blessed constantly by the running water, or to bless it. In one sculpture, dry in this season, Vishnu, supported by the serpent Ananta ("the Infinite"), floats on the Ocean of Milk, dreaming the cosmos into being, while his consort Lakshmi massages his legs. Not long before my visit, thieves had crudely hacked out the figure of Lakshmi to sell on the black market.

Cheth was still on the phone. It seemed that the American woman wanted to hire him, but his English was not strong enough, and he could only tell her to call the front desk of our hotel to make arrangements. Then the front desk called: it had been my wife, calling from New York to tell us that her father had died, eight days after I left him, from pneumonia. As he faded away, my sister-in-law had played her flute in his hospital room.

It is written in the *Katha Upanishad* that one should draw out the thumb-sized spirit from the body just as one does the wind from a reed. For a parent who has felt the supreme vulnerability of the soft spot on an infant's head, this account of death has a wonderful symmetry to it. A note in the translation by S. Radhakrishnan directs the reader to a parallel passage in the *Chandogya Upanishad*, and explains:

"It is said, that if a man has lived the disciplined life of a student and so 'found the self,' then at the time of death, his soul, dwelling in the heart, will pass upward by an artery known as *suṣumnā* . . . to an aperture in the crown of the skull known as the *brahmā-randhra* or *vidṛti*, by which at the beginning of life it first entered. For there the soul rises by the sun's rays to the sun which is the door-way to the Brahmā world to those who know and a stopping-place for those who do not know. The other ways lead the unliberated to re-embodiment."

In the National Museum at Phnom Penh

Was it in the infinite grace of Prajñāpāramitā,
    the Mother of all Buddhas
    imagined in the form of a child,
tranquil in gray sandstone for nine hundred years,
    that it finally came to me
    that you are gone from the world?

A young woman gave me a sliver of bamboo
    wrought up with white hyacinth
    and tipped with purple clover.
I inhaled its sweetness and returned that breath
    as an offering to you,
    not knowing where you are.

But as the rays of the Bodhisattva once
    entered his mother's body,
    making her feel as if
she embraced the whole world, some impulse of mercy
    inhabited the silence,
    articulating grief,

. . .

so that, in the child squatting to defecate

    (his mother solicitous,

    dabbing the ancient stone

of the cruciform cloister with a blue tissue)

    one morning at Angkor Wat,

    I knew you had been reborn.

IV.

For five years, one of my older half brothers has lived on an ashram in the Indian state of Uttaranchal, near the source of the Ganges, near where the goddess Parvati waited for her husband Lord Shiva and created the jolly, elephant-headed god Ganesh to keep her company. My brother has been involved in the Transcendental Meditation movement since 1973, the year after our mother died at the age I am now, forty-nine. I suspect that somehow her early death, combined with the trauma of the Vietnam War—which he actively opposed—propelled him into TM. As he explains it (in a multicultural pun), there was a boulder in his life-stream until a roc swooped down, as if from *The Arabian Nights*, and grabbed him. He now lives in a community of celibate and vegetarian males. YOU SHOULD ABANDON ORIGINS, says the motto. Perhaps my brother has succeeded in doing so.

According to a post-Vedic schema, there are four stages of life: the Student; the Householder, who raises and cares for a family;

the Forest Dweller, who lives in seclusion and cultivates a more spiritual life; and the Wandering Ascetic, the *sannyasin*, who has renounced all worldly possessions and seeks the liberation of his spirit from the cycle of rebirth. My brother seems to have passed from Student to Forest Dweller without ever having been a Householder. There is no *requirement* that one should go through all four stages, and my brother feels no loss. I cannot yet bring myself to think of him as a Wandering Ascetic (he is only fifty-six), though when my family and I moved into our first house in the Philadelphia suburbs two years ago, he gave us a great deal of the beautiful handmade furniture that had filled his apartment on an ashram in North Carolina. He had not been in that apartment in years, yet in an e-mail he described each piece of furniture in loving detail, suggesting that he had indeed known how to live in the ordinary world. Why must I read his retirement from it as a renunciation? He said he was ready to simplify his life.

A Prayer to Ganesh

On West Ninety-sixth Street, outside the Ayurveda Center,
    dirty snow still dimples the god's bronze thighs
where he sits, plump as a *gulab jamun* in rosewater,
    a delight to his mother Parvati in her cave of ice.

First-worshipped, fashioned out of her skin's gold dander,
    lord of servants and elephant-headed keeper of doorways,
liminal god between the past and the future
    who removes obstacles or sets them in place,

. . .

smiling portmanteau god who, in father and mother,
    found and circled the entire universe,
incline toward me the gray fan of your ear.
    Return him from the exile of Lord Shiva's

terrible rage for intelligence and order,
    from the *shakti* of a mother who never dies.
Bring him back from where Ganga threads from the glacier.
    Release him from the austerity of his prayers,

from the loneliness of his concentration, or
    make me the single mind equal to his,
though I write with a broken tusk on birch-bark, far
    from the fields of eternal balance where he is.

Once a year my brother comes down off his mountainside for medical and dental checkups in the nearest city. This year I met him in Delhi, and we traveled together to Rishikesh, on the Ganges, where he had arranged for what is called a *pitri tārpana*, a ceremony for our dead ancestors. *Pitri* in Sanskrit means "father" or "forefather"; from the same Indo-European root come the Latin *pater*, German *Vater*, and so on. A *tārpana* is refreshment with libations of water. (There is another ceremony, the *pitri yagya*, in which the ancestors are offered a full meal, with a leaf dish set out for each ancestor by name. It is a responsibility of the Householder to feed them regularly.)

A ceremony in honor of dead ancestors could hardly be inappropriate, I thought. My mother, in particular, has dominated all of us by her black Scots presence, even as my father has dominated me by his passiveness and reticence. My mother was a poet, of the generation of Plath and Sexton and Rich, trapped in a set of assumptions about the role of women from which she escaped only through alcohol and early death, if not through the lives of her children and her poems. It cannot be an accident that I have become a poet, determined to follow her vocation further than she was able to do.

To conduct the ceremony, my brother had found a Tamil pandit (a wise or learned man) in Rishikesh named K. R. A. Subramaniam, a gentle, gray-haired man with a face of such kindness that the problem of a common language seemed almost irrelevant. He spoke little English; we spoke no Hindi or Tamil. Having left his family in the south, Pandit Subramaniam lived alone in a couple of dark rooms. Though he was the head priest of the Chandra Mouli Swami temple, consecrated to Shiva, one of his rooms boasted a large wall calendar bearing the image of Venkateshwara, an incarnation of Vishnu for this Kali Yuga, this wicked age in which we live. Venkateshwara is depicted blindfolded, lest the *darshan* (power acquired by looking) from his gaze incinerate the worshipper. Indeed, the Shiva temple and the Venkateshwara temple in Rishikesh are next door to each other, and the priest we saw tending to the *murtis* (idols) in the Shiva temple wore on his forehead the three vertical marks that identified him as a Vaishnavite, while Pandit Subramaniam wore the three horizontal marks of a Shaivite. But then, it is said that the lifetime of Vishnu equals a hundred lifetimes of Brahma, and of Shiva a hundred lifetimes of Vishnu, and of Devi (the divine mother) a hundred lifetimes of Shiva: so the gods contain one another like nesting dolls.

Pandit Subramaniam accompanied us through the streets of Rishikesh to a ghat on the west bank of the Ganges. He was disturbed when a black dog crossed our path, fearing this to be a bad omen. It was February—spring in northern India—and the weather was perfect, like March in Rome or April in Pennsylvania. Pandit Subramaniam wore a *dhoti* (cloth for the lower-body), tied South Indian style, but also a Northern Indian *kurta* (upper-body covering sewn into a long-tailed shirt) and a shawl: a hybrid attire intended to cope with what he, as a southerner, found to be chilly weather. I was wearing a pair of incongruous crimson bathing trunks under the hand-loomed *lungi* (sheetlike lower-body covering) and *kurta* that my brother had presented to me, together with a long garland of marigolds, at the airport in Delhi. I had been instructed not to wear pants, but rather a seamless garment to correspond to the seamlessness of existence asserted by the ceremony. I felt naked and ill at ease.

The time and the place of the ceremony were both significant. We had been given to understand that the hours between noon and three were particularly auspicious for refreshing the *pitris*. Both Rishikesh and Haridwar, farther downstream, are considered auspicious places because there the Ganges is just leaving its divine source in the Himalayas and entering the Indian plains.

The ceremony began with our bathing in the purifying waters of the Ganges while the pandit chanted Sanskrit mantras over us. Of course I had no idea what he was saying; I was chiefly aware of how cold the water was, just out of the mountains. I had braved the waters of Deer Isle, Maine, for several summers in a row, but never for very long. I wondered when I would lose all feeling below my waist, and hoped it would be soon. The ceremony calls for complete immersion (including the head) a minimum of three times. I thought of the "clear gray icy water" of Nova Scotia, which Elizabeth Bishop described as a matrix of suffering and knowledge. At least I had the presence of mind to palm off the three mouthfuls of Gangajal the ceremony required that I swallow.

The next part of the ceremony was the *sankalpa*, the "intention," which locates the *yajamana* (the one who has contracted for the ceremony) in cosmological time and place, as well as by name and Vedic lineage. An Indian would not think of himself as being a "Hindu"; rather, he would identify himself by his Vedic lineage and by the god(s) he specifically honors. (All foreigners are thought to descend from the primordial sage Kashyapa.) The *sankalpa* fixes one's temporal location in terms of a recurring Puranic cycle lasting trillions of years—a system well beyond the intellectual reach of one who cannot even figure the gas mileage of his Honda without a calculator. What interested me, however, was the 4:3:2:1 ratio of the four *yugas*, which was the same ratio I had paced out at Angkor Wat. The *sankalpa* also located my brother and me at an exact point in astronomical space, including our place on earth as defined by the rising sign of the zodiac. And it stated our names. The purpose of such detailed identification was to ensure that our *pitris* would be the ones to receive the offerings, and that the merit of the ceremony accrued to us.

The *pitris* are said by some to live in the south, which is the direction of Lord Yama. (In *The Mahabharata*, Yama loops his silver thread around the thumb-sized spirit of Prince Satyavat, withdraws it from its place near Satyavat's heart, and sets off to the south, with Satyavat's wife Savitri following him.) But others believe that the *pitris* inhabit the region of the air, and still others that they dwell in one of the twenty-seven or -eight mansions of the moon, in its progress through the heavens. Pandit Subramaniam called our ancestors by name—the only part of the ceremony I understood—to come from the air above the southern horizon and to enjoy the refreshments we were offering them, although he instructed us to face north, toward the mountains and the source of the Ganges, so that the river would be on our right. If my ancestors *did* come from the south, I may have missed their arrival.

The *pitris* are always hungry, and therefore are prone to be irritable and intolerant of mistakes. It might have been for this reason, rather than merely because of my clumsiness and illiteracy, that Pandit Subramaniam seemed tense. For it is the pandit, and not the person who pays for the ceremony, who is liable for any mispronunciations of the mantras or mistakes in the ritual, and who presumably will pay in the hereafter.

We were to give the *pitris* Gangajal to drink and black sesame seeds to eat, these things offered with the right hand. All my life I have believed in the symbolic power of rivers, and in their combinative power where they join: the Sihl and the Limmat at Zurich, for example, or the Rhône and the Arve at Geneva. The Ganges, of all rivers, makes life whole and fecund. As for the black sesame seeds, they are said to be particularly enjoyed by the *pitris*. They symbolize the unbroken loop of consciousness as nourishment fed by the living to the dead, consciousness becoming manifest and returning to the unmanifest, feeding itself to itself. The intimacy of the relationship between the living and the dead here seems to me like that whereby one finally recognizes that the *darshan* from an idol or a saint is that of the self, because in looking at the *murti* the worshipper is looking at a single self.

As is the case in India for any event, ordinary or extraordinary, a crowd had gathered to watch the ceremony. I found myself kneeling on the ghat with sacred *kusha* grass wound between the fingers of my right hand. (Savitri sat on a cushion of *kusha* grass when she went to live with her in-laws in the forest. Its blade has a sharp tip, and someone of penetrating and shrewd intelligence is said to have a mind like *kusha* grass.) I filled my cupped palm with Gangajal from a brass bowl and, with a flick of the wrist and a kind of hitchhiking motion, tossed the water back into the river. The word *pitri* also refers to the part of the hand between the thumb and forefinger, which is sacred to the *pitri*s; so the water's passing between thumb and forefinger ensured that it would reach the ancestors and refresh them.

My brother and I repeated this motion with palmfuls of black sesame seeds. At last we flung away even the *kusha* grass woven between our fingers, and I discovered that I was in tears. We got up off our aging knees. We gave *dakshina* (payment for a sacred performance) to Pandit Subramaniam, traditionally consisting of a towel, a shawl, a cloth for the lower body and one for the upper, something of metal such as a *thali* (an eating dish), several pieces of fruit, and finally some cash—though never an even amount, for only odd numbers are auspicious.

Perhaps the ceremony *did* nourish our ancestors, but I felt no closer to them at that moment than I had to my uncle when I was on

Saipan. According to the Puranas, a year in the life of the living is like a day in the life of the dead. My uncle has been gone only sixty days, I thought. He is twenty-two, not eighty-three. He is younger than I am, and I long to see him, to know what he will make of his life. My mother is still middle-aged, and perhaps she will find her way back to poetry, after a few more years of parenthood.

The next evening we attended a Ganga Aarti, a ceremony honoring the goddess of the Ganges, in Haridwar. This ceremony is famous for the little boats, made of *bilba* leaves held together with toothpicks and filled with flowers and camphor lights, that are launched on the river at sunset. These little boats seem overwhelmingly frail as they are released. It was our own family we were witnessing; it was the spirits of my father and mother, of my uncle and grandmother, and of my father-in-law that I watched bob dauntlessly away into the dusk.

V.

There is a final motto at the feet of the Buddha, once again spelled out in rounded river stones: YOU SHOULD ATTAIN CESSATION. The Buddha means by this that we should attain deliverance from rebirth; but I will settle for calm in the face of the devouring past. I girdled the earth to complete a pilgrimage—or a *yatra*, as Hindus

call it—that the dead did not require of me, but that I neverthe-
less felt compelled to make.

Eventually I did dream my own death: at one point during the trip,
I had a nightmare in which I watched the left wing of the plane
in which I was traveling break off just as it touched down on the
runway.

According to the *Upanishads*, the dream world lies beyond the
waking world of the senses, and beyond that is "the bliss and free-
dom of dreamless sleep." Beyond *that* is the "illuminated" freedom
of *purusha*, or pure consciousness, the fourth state, which is im-
mortal. My brother describes this beautifully: the first three states
are like translucent curtains drawn across the shining screen of the
fourth, and they come and go endlessly.

My father knew nothing of these four states of consciousness.
I remember sitting with him near the end of his life, in the park-
ing lot of an A&P in the Connecticut suburbs. After a pause in
which I realized that I had no idea what we were really talking
about, or what would come next, he said that he imagined death
would be like a dreamless sleep. I was profoundly moved. He
had always seemed so stubbornly mundane, in his devotion to
those around him, that it never occurred to me that he had given
the afterlife any thought.

When I was safely home, my eight-year-old daughter dreamed that I had died, and came in tears in the middle of the night to join us in bed. My wife and I said to each other that she was working through the loss of her grandfather.

A neighbor brought us a stoppered bottle of maple syrup, "because you should have something sweet," and I thought again of the palm sugar that I did not taste that day on a dusty road in Cambodia.

Waking After One Month Away

The spring is not yet very far advanced.
    Visible through the gray
branches, the traffic moves west on Route 30,
    a punctilio of ruby

taillights, purposeful into the sunset.
    But always in my dream
they rise, the crumbling sweat-stained terraces.
    I am in the deep fosse

with gods and demons avid for each other.
    Here Vishnu, as a lion,
mauls the Asura king. He grips the trembling
    limbs, the sexual part,

the smiling lips, the eyes that turn inward.
    And although, when I wake,

behind the window's three plain wooden crosses
the light is undeceived,

a wash of northern silver, for an instant,
just like the plume of snow
the jet stream lifts from the brow of Himavant,
these will not let me go.

"The two dark messengers of Yama with flaring nostrils wander among men, thirsting for the breath of life," go the verses in the *Rig Veda*. They fill me with despair: I will never escape from Dharma and Chitragupta, from the famished attention of the ancestors; I cannot fill the absence. But then I read on: "Let them give back to us a life of happiness here and today, so that we may see the sun." Even so, Lord Yama finally gave back to Princess Savitri her husband Satyavat.

Though it was westward, my progress from Saipan to Cambodia to India returned me eventually to the family I had left, to a family altered by death but still substantially intact and miraculously alive. I traveled in the direction of death, but returned to the only life I have been able to make. For unlike both my uncle and my brother, I am a Householder. That is my place.

NOTES

"The Happiness of This World"
Christophe Plantin was a French-born printer who lived and worked in
Antwerp, where today there is a museum bearing his name.

"Reading Akhmatova"
A palate expander (glued in place) is now a standard element of ortho-
dontia. It is adjusted by means of a key.

"A Sonata of Biber's"
Heinrich Ignaz Biber (1644–1704) composed a series of sonatas for
violin, based on the Rosary; each sonata required that the violin be tuned
differently (and in one the D and A strings are actually crossed behind
the bridge), in a practice known as *scordatura.* The Latin title of the sec-

ond movement of Sonata XI (called "The Resurrection," part of the
Five Glorious Mysteries) translates as "Christ Is Risen Today."

"At Giacometti's Grave"

The italicized lines in this poem are quotations of Alberto Giacometti
taken from James Lord's *Giacometti: A Biography* (1985). The poem bor-
rows other details from Lord's biography.

"Quiet Like the Fog"

This poem combines (antiphonally) details from events in Falluja, Iraq,
in April 2004 with lines from the bass recitative "Am Abend, da es kühle
war" in Bach's *Saint Matthew Passion*. The poem's title is a phrase provided
by the U.S. military to describe the movement of American troops.

"Val Veddasca"

The Italian epigraph translates roughly as "The owner's eye makes the
garden more beautiful." The valley referred to is in Italy and leads to
Lago Maggiore.

"The Names"

The opening quotation is from DeVoto's edition of *The Journals of Lewis
and Clark* (1953; reprinted, with foreword by Stephen E. Ambrose, Boston:
Houghton Mifflin, 1999). The poem is set in Big Timber, Montana.

"Tynnichus of Chalcis"

He is mentioned in Plato's short dialogue *Ion*.

"A Yatra *for Yama"*

My brother and I celebrated my birthday in February 2005 at the Maharaja Palace Hotel in Bharatpur, India (in fact, we dined under a portrait of the last Maharaja of Bharatpur), and he presented me with two volumes I have quoted from in this memoir: *The Rig Veda: An Anthology,* selected, translated, and annotated by Wendy Doniger O'Flaherty; and *The Principal Upaniṣads,* edited with introduction, text, translation, and notes by S. Radhakrishnan.

ABOUT THE AUTHOR

Karl Kirchwey is the author of four earlier volumes of poetry: *A Wandering Island, Those I Guard, The Engrafted Word* (a *New York Times* Notable Book for 1998), and *At the Palace of Jove*. Formerly director of the Unterberg Poetry Center of New York City's 92nd Street Y, he is now an associate professor and director of the creative writing program at Bryn Mawr College. His poetry has appeared in publications including *The New Republic, The Paris Review, Parnassus, The New Yorker, The New York Review of Books,* and *Slate.* Among the honors he has received are the Norma Farber First Book Award, grants from the National Endowment for the Arts and from the Ingram Merrill and John Simon Guggenheim Memorial foundations, and the Rome Prize in Literature. He lives in Wayne, Pennsylvania, with his wife and their two children.